Dear December

cincity G

BookLeaf Publishing

India | USA | UK

Presentation by *BookLeaf Publishing*

Web: www.bookleafpub.com

E-mail: info@bookleafpub.com

ISBN: 9789357697071

First edition 2023

DEDICATION

To those who stand behind Love.

ACKNOWLEDGEMENT

I have had some ignorant people in my life and I want to thank you for being you!
If not for you - I never would have found my knowledge, my soul family, my tribe, my truth.

PREFACE

If I speak in the tongues of men or of angels, but do not have love, I am only a resounding gong or a clanging cymbal. If I have the gift of prophecy and can fathom all mysteries and all knowledge, and if I have a faith that can move mountains, but do not have love, I am nothing. If I give all I possess to the poor and give over my body to hardship that I may boast, but do not have love, I gain nothing.

Love is patient, love is kind. It does not envy, it does not boast, it is not proud. It does not dishonor others, it is not self-seeking, it is not easily angered, it keeps no record of wrongs. Love does not delight in evil but rejoices with the truth. It always protects, always trusts, always hopes, always perseveres.

Love never fails. But where there are prophecies, they will cease; where there are tongues, they will be stilled; where there is knowledge, it will pass away. For we know in part and we prophesy in part, but when completeness comes, what is in part disappears. When I was a child, I talked like a child, I

thought like a child, I reasoned like a child.
When I became a man, I put the ways of
childhood behind me. For now, we see only a
reflection as in a mirror; then we shall see face
to face. Now I know in part; then I shall know
fully, even as I am fully known.

And now these three remain: faith, hope and
love. But the greatest of these is love.

1 Corinthians 13

Dear December,

Dear December,
The journey far and wide.
Dear December,
The beginning and end at the same damn time.

It is not too often,
Do we have the chance and time to grow.
December, the cold and dark,
Time to internalize and snow!

I want each month,
Each day to be better.
Then again, December,
Some nights, I don't want to remember.

The lessons, mine alone;
Happy, sad, and in between.
I project. I learn. I grow.
Everything was meant for me.

Thank you December,
I thank you for your truth.
I innerstand.
I heal.
I know all is, me times two.

The lesson, our spirits calling,
No life is the same.
Once you see, each day we crawling
And when we learn to walk, the world can no
longer tame.

I am grateful and protected,
Ready to bloom!
Dearest December,
Not a real month but, each minute,
Each breath, is my story to consume.

Dear Mom,

I never asked to be here.
Mom, I am your karma.
The love you showed, just unclear.
Why have me for the drama?
Most children created for love,
A concept so unseen.
Growing up was hard and rough,
Wanting for a momma to believe.
Believe in me, support,
Show me how to move.
This world is full of friends and fakes.
Mom, I wanted to look up to you.
But you were just as broken,
Had no business in charge of my soul.
Mom, each word unspoken,
Your version of love was fucked up,
But that's all you'd known.
We are all born with traumas,
You thought you'd pass yours down.
This time I am aware. I innerstand. I heal.
I am love, inside and out.
I know you didn't know,
How to show me the love I needed.
Sorry for what they said to you,
You're fucking dope, I wish you'd see it.

May we see with a new light,
I love you for where we've been.
Today I will fight, it's bigger than you,
These curses stop in this generation.
You called me the black sheep constantly,
Means I carry a new code of survival.
Mom, see me moving differently?
I made this promise upon arrival.

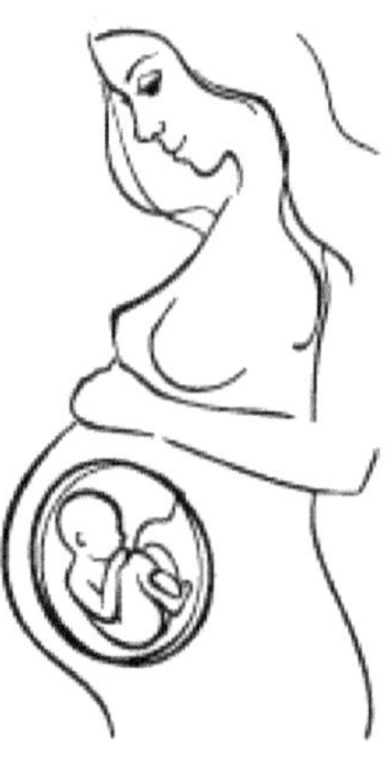

Dear Dad,

I see you strong soldier,
The world is on your back.
And as you grow older
Dad, do you know you never lacked?

Mom's stories of you,
Deadbeat, good for nothing, coward, weak.
Gems the world says has to be true,
I saw you work for us, losing hours of sleep.

I watched you daily, going to work in a world
That looks at you sideways.
You put in hours for bare minimum, no maybes,
In a place where the "master" moves in
Prescribed ways.

Dad, stop choosing to be blind.
I know your struggles, they don't treat you right.
We need your protection, you built mankind.
We are right behind you if you choose to fight.

Move *that* mentality to the side,
You are needed and we love you.
Our spirit is here just for a ride.

Soul divine, God-like, and that's why they hate
times two.

I want you to know, Dad, you are important
And breaking your spirit was part of the plan.
No golden child is weak nor dormant.
They undermine our mental, steal our IP, and
then "lend a hand".

Well, that mentality is over,
Bent Dad, never broken.
You've always been my hero, soldier.
With the world on your shoulder,
We speak, words unspoken.

You built everything from ground zero.
You built our home. You are the foundation.
Show me strength, let's level up, no Nero,
Inherit King, of all nations.

Dear Broken Children,

Each day worse than the next,
Maybe stop saying I'm blessed.

Words cast spells, it's time to see.
Not blessed as in "blessed" rather be-less,
It's a spell on your mentality.

I want to let you in on a secret,
Promise me you will not keep it.

They know your power and move in fear.
So they kill, be-little, and be-lack cuz they
scared.

Let me repeat, these words cast spells, we need
to care.
We are no longer lacking, on this side here.

You see be-lack is not a color, but a mind frame.
A spell we cast thinking black and brown are
one in the same.
Innerstand duality is the name of this game.

White vs Black,
Trust it is right vs lack.
A program in the matrix I promise to re-rap.
We finna talk about it and set this shit back.

Broken but not shattered,
Bent and never bruised.
God told you who matters,
And who to look up to.

Trust no word of man.
You see, Hollywood is full of fakes.
No weapon formed can withstand,
God has his children in a safe place.

Remember your power and move,
You have been lied to for 400 years.
Now it's time to rewind the confuse,
In the end, courage overrides fear.

As God's children,
Know who your creator be.
Protected, abundant, creative,
powerful, important, Earth's native,
inventors of all,
And that's the real mentality.

Dear Broken Queen,

Society wants you light,
I mean white - straight hair, clean eyes.
The creator knows what's right.
You see the sun, that is the fuel for you to
survive.

Dear Queen,
You are that and soul much more.
Divine feminine you see,
All you were made to bore?
For you are the foundation of future Kings and
Queens, but who is keeping score?

Hold your head with such grace,
This is your birthright.
I know it gets hard in the matrix,
But the ancestors say fight.

You're broken not shattered,
Means your experiences shaped you.
And those that mind, don't matter.
Honestly evolving is part of your truth.
The courage to live broken, bold, and
be-you-too-full.

Queen, that is your story.
You find the power and strength within.

And trust the process,
Preach God Be the Glory.
You are a wolf, time to shed the sheepskin.

Stop comparing yourself to theirs,
God had you in His laboratory.
You must see all the ways you have proved
You're so worthy, let's check the inventory.

Show 'em Queen what you made of,
God made zero mistakes.
Will you learn from the experience
Or let the world force you flat on your face?

The world needs you, Queen, remain strong,
You must show your sons who they are.
No more bowing down, stop singing sob songs,
Together we'll rise and see the stars.
See, Queen was never broken, just believing
bullshit all along,
Now, let's finish patching up these scars.

Dear Broken King

Hi King, do you remember me?
It is your Queen, here to remind you of all you
used to be.
Not a dream,
I know he broke you mentally
-or so it seems,
But do you know who your creator be?

The Most High made a covenant,
For this is his creation.
Made with His children from Israel.
With a people, not a nation.

Here you sit in a state of confusion,
Incomplete but you're enough.
Stop seeing just the optical illusion,
It's time to call their bluff.

You are not this body.
Time to see past Jezebel and her sexuality.
In this world your mind has got to stay strong,
And this is how you change your reality?

Your heart broken, bruised, and told you were
not worthy.
King, your Queen is here to stand with you,
But the protection and respect are concerning.

How can you save me if you hurt me so?
We need love and respect then, gracefully,
Can we come together and grow?

Fall down nine, King, get up ten,
This is what our Father commands.
We are here. We are not them.
We are His children and will inherit the land.
Move different and see this is yours, your
king-dam,
To be reclaimed by man.
In the past we rose and have fallen,
And now a new plan!
This time, we finally holding hands.

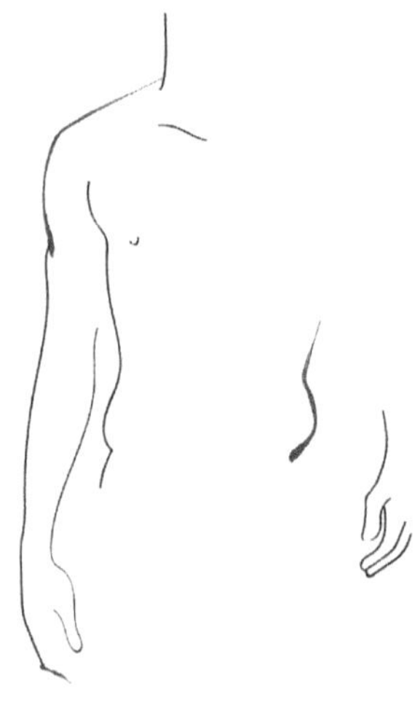

Dear Hue-Mans,

There's a difference between me and you,
It goes deeper than the melanin.
The facts are in our truth.
Of who is Israel, God's children.
And yes it is important I said who not where,
Please read our history, get a clue,
Wake up, it's time to care.

Hue-mans, how literal can you be?
You know God's language is numerology?

All truths can be found in the numbers,
Break down white and black and see
polarity succumbs us.

It is what it is, opposites on a spectrum.
It is what it is, 400 years of mental Slavedom.

No better is any man, not a quarter, nor barely
whole.
We are simply shades of hues, man,
We've been lied to. Truth hidden for centuries,
Blind fish swimming in no bowl.

All hues are God's children, some more than
others.

Free will and shining -
We cause beauty and scars.

Nothing a mistake, so together we must lead.
You know the color red – the color all our
bloods bleed.

White is not better,
Black does not exist.
Again, it's merely the absorption of color,
A creation of split.
It's all energy and polar opposites.

May we come together to see,
Man with no hue.
God said he would create man in his image,
Just look at what the body do.
I leave this here not saying much, simply
speaking God's truth.
That sun, my skin, the Earth's creations,
See how the world is man's hue?

Dear Chosen Ones,

Knowing the journey would not be easy
just worth it,
Going through drama, dating the sleazy,
Like I deserve this.

Always out of place, never fitting in.
Looked at like a pure disgrace,
This is the life we live.

Being who you are is not easy, but necessary.
For you, your views of the world are far from
elementary.
The out-of-the-box, Black Sheep,
Always feeling lost, a bit incomplete.

You, Chosen King and Queen,
These life choices and experiences,
Shaped all of you for the healing you will bring
and that is what experience is.
Don't you dare believe a single thing.
The devil lies and wants evil to ring.
And he will not stop until he's ruined
everything.

And this is your purpose.
Here to bring peace and love to all,
For they deserve it.

Here to remind the world we are one,
Our birthright is the permit.

These trials and tribulations,
Always turn into triumphs and better
foundations.

Dear Chosen One, do you see your strength?
Do you see that we are all one in the same?
There is peace to inner stand, the world is the
twin flame.

A direct representation of the work you have
done.
The peace internal, creates the external sun.
Shine bright and stand into the glory of one.
As we move, we subdue,
All the evilest of bums.
You are stronger than you'd dream you'd ever
become.
Stand in truth.
God's got you,
Together we will improve and the game shall be
WON.

Dear Aaron,

So many words unspoken,
So much left unsaid.
I told you I loved you so many times,
But only in my head.

Thinking we had time,
Minutes, days, and years.
If the clock, I could rewind,
Wipe away your momma's tears.

It's hard, Aaron,
King, gone too soon.
I notice, God is taking back his soldiers,
Make sure you fix our room.

Gone and not forgotten,
The plans we fucking had.
Again, all my words unspoken,
We were going to create the dopest podcast.

I move in your name,
You showed me so much of a life.
Crazy to think how much your young self did
impact,
Your spirit was so might.

I see you, I feel you King.
You are here as energy.
Remember your theory?
I would've kept you in my simulation for
eternity.

I love you bro, I love you.
Thank you for your time.
My King you couldn't begin to know your
impact,
Your life still soul divine.

Dear Family,

Born unto people
That I never felt the love.
Yes, I had a mom and dad,
And still I was never enough.
A struggle of belonging and such,
The youngest of the bunch.
The idea that I was the "code'"
I didn't have it rough.

For a 3D life, I had all I need,
Roof over my head, food, heat, and weed.
Siblings, cousins, so much family and friends,
But something inside was always missing.
The picture of "family" I had in my head.

I choose this, fact of the matter,
I wanted the experience.
Of this mother, this father,
Now in the season of Aquarius.

The choices I made,
I am here with a purpose.
The future I seek,
Begins and ends in deservedness.

Born into a family where I can't seem to
"behave".
To a mom who judges,
a soul I can't save.

I now look at this family with new loving eyes.
Difficult or easy we will build,
With grace and no more cries.

Dear Soul Family,

A family unit I created
And a vibe based on emotions.
My soul family, we finally made it,
We swam through many oceans.

You are my tribe, we came down to this place,
Scattered and alone.
And our journeys, none the same,
But they brought us here for the mome-
For the moment of creation,
To push you to your path.
I know I almost didn't make it,
Thinking that moment, that feeling would last.

I'm happy for the family I had and now have
lost.
Looking back, I realize, they came at a heavy
cost.

I know now what it is,
What's the family that I need?
A soul family that's there always,
No judgment, just cheerlead.
One that won't stab you till you bleed,
Talk shit, make you feel less than, and leave.

That's not the right people to keep.

I have learned many lessons and now I can see.
I see my past triumphs led me to you sis, mom,
dad.
Praises for my soul family!

Dear Future Husband,

Almost ready give me a few,
I am becoming my best version.
I thought I was in love and had found you,
I had no idea that was a diversion.

Jezebel is real, an enemy of deceit.
She is coming for everything you got.
I've been lied to left and right in these streets,
Not realizing they steal parts.
They took parts of me without a second thought,
Replacing steel in missing pieces of my heart.

As I put me back together to be,
In the best shape of my life.
I have no regrets, each memory,
A piece in the cincity strife.
Praise God for getting me ready,
I've seen the fuck boy from all sides.
I know who I am and I am worthy.
The King on my path is my soul's wife!

A relationship so sacred, it's dharmic in a way.
Created by the divine for our souls to shine,
He can be found at Heaven's Gate,
One would even claim fate.

I am ready God and I thank you, for my
protector in the flesh.
Together I know magic will happen,
I deserve more and nothing less.

I am now all I came to be and some.
Dear Husband, thank you for being patient.
I know everything we will overcome,
Together with communication.

One in the same, we think alike,
This is something I am not accustomed.
May I be the better half of this man,
Thank you for coming to me,
Thank God for my Future Husband.

Dear Young Queen,

Bitch bad, woman good,
Seems like everyone has an opinion.
That song's perspective by Lupe
Made me see we one of OR one in one million.

See Queen, the choice is yours,
Do what you see or what you know.
Baby girl, plant your seeds of love,
Learning, inner standing, this is how we grow.

You're sexy, you're dope,
You make a baby out of one sperm.
You're worth more than gold,
Black Queen, stop giving up all your goods.
No reason to twerk,
There's more to your worth.
Fully covered up, bitch, you still look good.

We have been created for greatness,
Making houses into homes.
Then get sold all this fakeness,
Like Beyoncé cares for truth over
adrenochrome!
Care not does she, nor Cardi B,
We need better role models.

You ever ask yourself why, Black Queens,
Are never on the front of medicine bottles?

Worth more than gold,
Claim and say that twice!
It's the melanin of God placed over your soul.
Here on this Earth to be divine.
The future of humanity is in your control.
We are entering the end of time.

Queen, you are your King's counterpart,
Play accordingly, move differently.
We must leave the world better than we found,
We are breaking curses for eternity.

Breaking all mental chains.
The devil will not win this final round.
Our power is in knowing and proper gains.
Young Queen, do you see your ability to
compound?

To create, your capabilities
Are built in unity,
Now is not the time to divide.
Dear Young Queen, it's your part, your
soliloquy,
God is on your side.
The fake hues may now go under - it's their time
to hide.

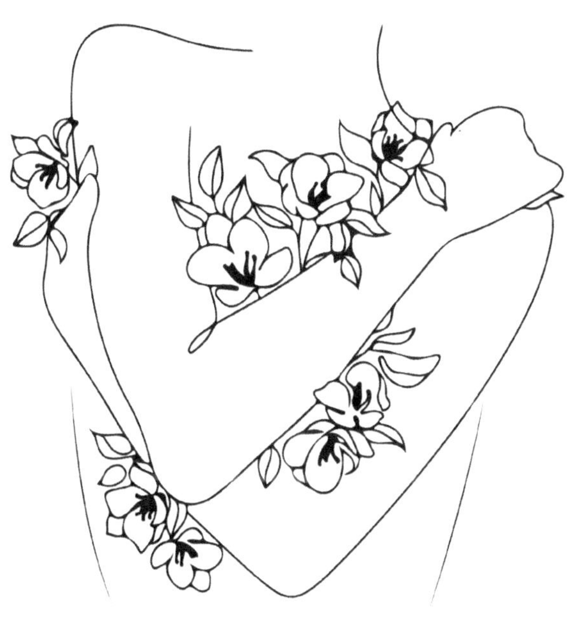

Dear Young King,

My King, I see you through the years,
Coming from shackles and overcoming fears.
All a journey for you to bear.
Truth or lie, it was your story to hear.
The chains, mental.
The handcuffs, oh, that's real.

Let's think, an entire people of gangsters and
thieves,
Means another race did this intentionally.
See King, when you stand in your power,
The ones that get scared, we call them cowards.
Those are the ones who see only color.

Otherwise Young King, Dear Child of God,
With the skin of brass and hair of wool cloth.
You are here to create and to be,
To be the hand of justice in this body.
King, now is the time, move accordingly.
Your Queen has been waiting, patiently.
Forced to be the head and the tail of the family.
Melanin worth more than gold, really Google
told me!

We can no longer fight any part of our soul.
Here to change the narrative, the world you will
show.
What a real man looks like and
How this nation will grow.
Young King, no longer weak,
Stand up – it's your Queen, with you fighting.
This is for all of hue-man-ity.

Dear Anon,

"I know you",
Better than I know myself.
Wise words spoken
From the spirit of Jezebel.
For you only knew the pieces
I placed on the shelf.
Act like that was all of me
And there was nothing else.
For I never shared 100% of me,
You never saw the top shelf.
But acted as if,
All my actions belonged in hell.

I will never forget the day you told me,
To move more positively.
Wise words coming from
The most negative thing.
Letting the words of one stranger
Ruin all life as it sings.
Then want to claim a family bond for
conveniences.

Na, girl you only knew what I wanted to show.
You also only knew a version of me that has
now grown.

I never fully let you in,
Family or not.
I simply showed you what I wanted,
So, you knew what you saw.
Never wanted to know more,
Just the surface of scars.
Or to keep me in a state of emotional imbalance,
Like a current-day Lazar.

Soul glad for the friendships
Or fakeness either way.
I had the experience
I wanted in this space.

Praise God for each and every moment of truth.
For I would not be me, if not for you.

Inner stand now,
As we are not the same.
Just know I played with you,
As part of the game.

Dear Future Child

I know just who you are
And what you're meant to be.
A manifestation of me and dad's karma,
In this time-space reality.
I used to be sad, upset,
You have yet come on to me,
But baby I am still becoming,
The mom you need me to be.

Once broken, I promise I am healing.
These shadows and traumas
Are mine for the feeling.
Dear Future Child, I know I am almost ready
To be the one you need.
I want to love you, unconditionally.
There will be zero tricks or hatred up any sleeve.

I am getting right, my future child,
We certainly will have work to do.
I promise to show you all I know
And I will learn from you too!
God praises to me
And especially unto you.

I promise to move in greater steps,
To show you the way and you can teach me the
rest.
We know there's work to do here on Earth.
God, my baby and I understand the assignment
and together we will work.

Born unto me and how grateful I am.
A perfect creature, magnificently,
I will protect and serve as the plan.

Thank you for showing up for me and loving me
with your heart.
Dear future child, I promise to be your guide on
Earth,
Until we are reunited with the source.

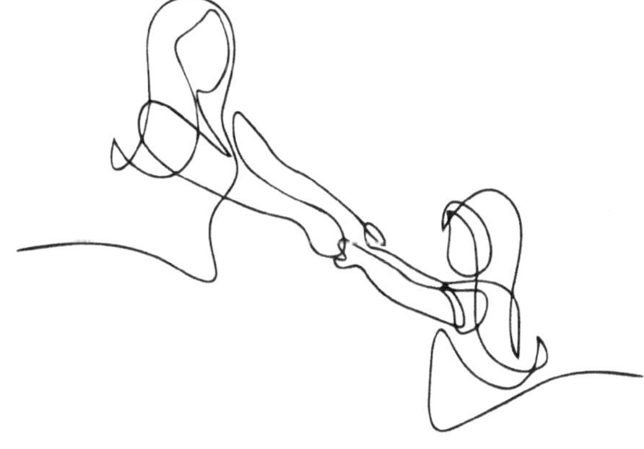

Dear Old Me,

You moved in a way,
Be it happy or sad.
Smile through the pain,
It was not that bad.
You carried an emotion,
One you never had to bear.
Stuck swimming in oceans,
Where no one even cared.
Old me, I thank you,
For those bits of desperation.
To show me how to move,
In a different vibration.
None of it's true,
Perspective, deception.
But, sometimes we can't,
See past our own reflection.
Never bitter, just better,
Each moment one that shaped me.
I survived and I matter,
I was created for greater things!
We will never forget,
The friends, good times, words spoken.
Now moving in silence,
God's promises are never broken.
We want those who want us,

And love with no conditions.
Remember all of them "broke" times?
Your thoughts had you missing.
Each moment created
By you, your environment.
I am happy I experienced,
I wouldn't change a thing.

Old Me, I thank you again,
So naïve and trusting.
I know there was divinity in each breakthrough.
To be here in this moment,
No more adjusting.

Dear Current Me,

We made a lot of discoveries,
The question is who to tell.
Say it intentionally,
So it may be received well.
How far you have come,
A few more steps to go.
You carried yourself with such grace,
Some haters will never know.
A reflection I will be,
So you can see who you are.
A mirror to be clear,
You're a powerful entity of God.

I know all that I am.
I forgot who I was.
Hard to believe the creeps lie,
To kids to "show" them who God loves.
Sorry, not sorry,
The time is now, it's time to innerstand.
Realize all your life choices,
Are at your own hand.
I love that I know,
This is all my fault.
A promise I made to learn,
A promise to evolve.
You were told your name,
Mom, dad, and weight,

Even your hometown experiences,
Nothing's a mistake.

Spirit knew and you promised,
To walk this path.
Knowing is forgetting,
The past and what you had.
A realization comes when
You stop crying and live.
Each moment, good and bad,
Was your experience.
Keep learning, keep growing,
You get up easier if you fall on your back.
A choice to be in the moment,
Thank God, I now know internal peace is all we
have.
Remain thankful and soul grateful.
The moves I need to make.
Dear Current Me, Thank you for showing me
who I am to be -
A promise of love in each day.

Dear Future Me,

"The Secret" told us the realization of time.
The past and future tenses are all in the mind.
The present is only a piece in the puzzle of
mankind.
Everything else a perception, only alive when
aligned.
In hindsight, you were there, on the mountain
climb.
The future, an idea, and in arrival you shall
shine.
This concept really blows my mind.
And is the case, so why,
Would we rather remain stuck and soul blind?

Dear Future Me, when we finally meet. I know I
am sublime.
I see the trenches and valleys, that our feet have
climbed.
Fake friend, real haters, all inside
My family, my circle and I never knew why.
Thank you for each dream planted in my mind.
Each waking morn was a struggle at times.
The journey of self and purpose is all in the
divine.

Soul grateful and thankful I always dried my
tears after each cry.
Alone, made fun of, not feeling love at times.
All I know is thank you for growth because I
have been lost inside.

Future Me, thank you for preventing the devil
from taking hold of my mind.
Praises for strength and Anaheim.
I know peace exists and harmony in the world is
via man, kind.
To the ones in the future,
Show me more glimpses so I am no longer
blind.
I am purpose, I am love, I am the greatest gift -
and now it's showtime.

Dear Love,

There is an emotion we long for,
Each and every day.
Dear Love, I want to feel you,
In the most grandiose and miniscule of ways.

This fuel we need, we yearn and weep
For each heartbreak brings us pain.
Never seeing all we have is all we need,
All we see is the pouring rain.

Love yourself first, no one ever told me this.
You are the equivalent of God,
So loving you is loving It.
Each breath is your reward.

In reality, the world is one big game,
Play wisely and lean with love.
Dear Love, may I be so with elegance and grace.
I know I am all that I am and in that I am
enough.

Love harder in times of hardship,
I love because it's God.
There is no black and white on Earth's ship.
Regardless of what is, I am the staff and the rod.

My eyes can see,
My heart will feel,
Only that which makes me dance.
Love isn't something money can buy
Or hidden in between our pants.

Love is kind,
Love is peace,
The bible tells you so.
Dear Love, thank you for loving me.
If you are looking for love in a world out there,
Becoming -
Is how you grow.

Dear God,

God, can I thank you?
The good and bad times shaped me.
I give thanks for where I been,
All in place for who I am to be.
I thank you,
Never saying it when sad, only when happy.
So now, I give thanks always,
For each reflection showed me how to see.
I strive to serve you in all ways,
As you have provided me with such grace and
harmony.

So grand of an Earth,
Where things seem to work.
Birds fly, lions roar,
Snakes sneak at birth.

God, each day is Grand,
Each thought a projection.
Each miracle is one of you,
Soul happy to spread your message.

To be here in this time and place.
My service to you is truth, love, and praise.
May I show you how amazing
I am through you.
May I rise to each occasion,
Continue living your truth.

God, I am so protected and abundant.
You are my rock and my Savior.
May I continue to push, survive, and thrive,
And lend a hand to my neighbor.

The world is changing,
God, I pray for our youth.
May your love shine in the corners of dark places.
Finally, with you, there is only truth.

Thank you for choosing me and filling all the
bases,
Happily I live and move in your plans.
The dreams I dream are yours and mine for the
making,
Equally, no more demands.

May I not take life too seriously.
My eyes are open,
And my heart is clean.
I promise to embody your truth,
With all of me.
Thank you for my protection and my life,
I am soul grateful for this spiritual journey.